Sanya's World

BOOK 1

Sanya's New Starts

Aditi Singh
Sharvi Singh

Paperback ISBN: 978-1-956870-06-0
Hardcover ISBN: 978-1-956870-07-7

THIS BOOK BELONGS TO

CONTENTS

SANYA'S NEW STARTS

ADITI W. SINGH'S NOTE

I couldn't believe it when Sharvi wrote three inspirational short stories and went onto win school and state writing competitions. The lessons within them inspired me so much with the value they provided to readers. It had taken me years to learn them myself and I decided to build them into a story that kids everywhere could enjoy and grow up with. Sharvi and I worked for months together developing the characters and adding more to the simple narratives that we had begun with. The joy I had in working with my daughter became the foundation of the Write to Publish program I started for kids around the world to share *their* culture and writing.

You can learn more about it on RaisingWorldChildren.com

This book is not only a mother-daughter journey but also an ode to those who desire social and emotional growth through self-reflection.

A huge thank you to all those who have picked up this and any of my other books, left a review, given feedback, shared my work with others, sent me DMs. I am always grateful for your time and choosing my words to sprinkle through your lives. Remember:

The only place you must first find belonging in this wacky world is within.

- Aditi Wardhan Singh

1 MORNING...

"Sanya, your dosa is ready." Dad called out, adding the rolled dosa and chutney to a plate. "Come quick, or you will say it's not crispy enough."

"Hold your horses! I'm here, Papa. Good morning." Sanya replied, sounding upset. She had dragged herself into the kitchen. She couldn't believe this dreaded day was finally here. She hugged her father and took her plate to the table, looking at her mom packing her lunch.

"Good morning, beta! Why did you take so long to come down?" Mom asked, adding a sandwich, apple, yogurt drink and Boondi laddoos to her lunch box.

Sanya made a face. "I was just sitting on my bed. I don't want to go to school," she said, plopping down onto the dining table chair with a frown.

She looked out the windows. The air was already cool, and a few leaves were turning orange. "I miss home." She sighed wistfully and corrected herself: "Our old home."

Sanya's mom put her baby brother Dev in his highchair and added some snacks to his tray.

He babbled. "Right Dev? The old house was so good, right!?" Sanya loved imagining what her baby brother might be thinking.

The baby cooed and smiled some more.

"Right! And all my friends were so nice too. You are so intelligent!"

The baby threw his bottle and some Cheerios on the floor.

"What a great idea. We should move back!" Sanya said as she picked up the Cheerios from the floor and looked hopefully at her parents.

Mom placed a glass of Turmeric milk in front of Sanya and smiled, "Everything new takes a while to get used to. You fell so much when you first started walking, and now look at you!"

Mom stretched her hands out and funnily exaggerated how Sanya went from waddling to walking. Sanya snorted on her milk, despite herself, but said, "Not funny! I was *two*! This is different. A new grade in a new place is different than toddling around!"

Dad added a dosa to Mom's plate and said, "You will be fine, beta. Before you know it, you will run down the school halls, knowing every nook and cranny. Creating chaos." He smiled kindly.

Sanya got up to put her plate and glass in the kitchen sink. She turned to look out the windows and took a deep breath. A tear escaped her eye. "I don't know anyone here." Her lips quivered.

Dad came over and hugged her. "We know it's hard. You have been so brave through the move. Helping out with baby Dev as much as you can."

"Someone had to help keep him from crying or rolling off the sofa. Right Dev?" Dev looked back at her blankly.

"Well! As they say, with the power of being a big sister come big responsibilities," Dad said, fists on his waist like Superman.

"With great power comes great responsibility is the quote, *and* that's from Spiderman." Sanya teased.

"I stand corrected and in gratitude for all you have done, my lovely, strong girl. For now, it's your responsibility to be brave and get to school on time."

Sanya filled her water bottle, packed her lunch box, slung her backpack over her shoulder, and headed out the door.

2 SCHOOL…

"Hello, I'm Sanya Singh," Sanya said to her teacher. The teacher smiled at her, "Saan-yaa Sing. I'm Mrs. Violet. What lovely long hair you have!"

"Thanks. Mom puts coconut oil in my hair every weekend." Sanya said, more loudly and brightly than she meant to. Mrs. Violet smiled and said, "How lovely. It certainly works for your hair."

Why did I say that? Sanya wondered, touching her hair, self-consciously pulling at the ends of her ponytail to tighten it. She walked to a chair and sat down. Her palms were sweaty, and her cheeks were on fire. Luckily, no one could see the weight on her heart.

Every step through the hallway of the new school had been hard as the sea of unknown faces engulfed her. The red brick walls were covered with affirmations and school rules. "Be yourself," one poster said. The other said, "Please adhere to school dress code regulations." It seemed contradictory, but that's life, she had thought.

Her mom had promised the move would be easy, but of course, it hadn't. This year has been weird. First came the baby, then she found out they were moving. Mom said there were more opportunities for creative people near the big city. The Big Apple is the true capital of America, she had said. Luckily, Sanya's dad worked from home, but moving all their stuff with baby Dev was chaotic. Leaving her friends was hard, and having a new brother was harder. Cute as a button, but what a magnet for Mom and Dad's time!

"Alright, class. Let me take a roll call." Sanya looked around as the kids were called, but so many new names didn't take, and they seemed to be staring at her. She felt them judging her: simple jumpsuit, brown eyes, wheat-ish skin tone, many bracelets, and her blue and red backpack.

Just as the roll call was over, a girl walked in with hair the color of autumn leaves and kind hazel eyes. Her soft features were in line with her pastel-colored dress. "Oh, hi! And who are you?" Mrs. Violet asked, looking over her student list.

"My name is Tonya." the girl replied, her eyes were glued to the floor.

"Tonya Muller! Welcome to our class. We have another new girl: Sanya. Sanya, Tonya. Tonya, Sanya. That almost rhymes. Haha." The kids laughed. Sanya wasn't sure if it was at their names or Mrs. Violet's attempt at humor. She didn't want to be talked about at all. She closed her eyes, took a deep breath through her nose, counted to five, and let it out through her mouth slowly. She did it three times. A practice her mom taught her when she would wake up crying in the new home many nights right after the move.

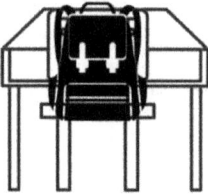

Feeling calmer, Sanya opened her eyes. She saw Tonya putting her book bag across the chair beside hers.

She noticed Tonya's lips quivering and shaking hands. Sanya felt guilty thinking this but was glad someone else was as scared as she felt.

3 ENEMY…

"Hi!" Sanya whispered. "Are you okay? I'm Sanya."

Tonya gave her a weak smile and whispered, "I don't like being around so many new people."

"Well, you are in luck! I have won prizes for making friends with everyone I meet with my awesome charm."

Tonya stared, mouth open, not knowing what to say when Sanya winked. Tonya smiled shyly at that.

Mrs. Violet clapped twice and pointed at the papers she had just given to the first child in the front row. "Let's go over class expectations. Please pass around this form for your parents to sign. When the bell rings, you go into Math. I hope you all have your schedules to keep track of the class you must go to next."

Sanya took out her schedule and looked across at Tonya, who was also looking at her sheet. Sanya showed her paper to Tonya, and they nodded, noticing they had math together. When the first bell rang, they walked side by side. Sanya didn't try to talk to Tonya but walked with her quietly.

"Hey!" A voice called from behind.

Sanya stopped and turned to see a tall girl with dazzling blonde hair like spun gold with eyes the color of emerald. "I'm Phoenix. I head the school newsletter." When Sanya smiled hello, she continued, "I have a question."

Sanya waited. "Does your mom grow her coconut trees in her backyard?" It took Sanya a moment to realize Phoenix was asking the question because of her reference to coconut oil. "No, we get it from the Indian store."

"Makes sense. It would certainly be hard to take care of coconut trees, right? You being so short and all." Sanya's mouth fell open.

"Do you know why the coconut went to school?" When Sanya didn't reply, Phoenix answered, "It wanted to be a smart nut. Like you, I guess." Laughing, Phoenix turned and walked away.

Sanya stood staring behind the girl she had never met before. Here went her streak of making friends with everyone she met. Oh well!

When she entered Math, her eyes found Tonya. She went and sat on an empty chair across the room. That little bitter exchange had made her late. She wished she could have sat with Tonya.

After 1.5 hours of math, it was time for recess. The bell rang. Sanya looked across the room, but Tonya had disappeared.

4 FRIEND…

Sanya walked out of the class and almost got run over by a million kids trying to get outside. When she finally found her way to the schoolyard, she looked everywhere for Tonya.

The ground looked like it was full of bees buzzing around. The sound was so loud yet joyful.

On one side, kids screeched as they played Gaga ball. In the smaller yard, boys played soccer, and in yet another place, kids were sitting in a circle just talking.

People surrounded Sanya, yet she felt all alone. She walked around, looking for someone to spend time with. She tried approaching a couple of groups sitting or standing in the grass, but they all just turned to stare at her.

When she found Tonya alone on a bench, she smiled. Sanya walked up to her and asked, "Why did you run off?"

"I wanted to beat the recess rush."

"Do you want to play with me?"

"Sure!" Tonya replied with a shrug. She stood up and started walking towards the track around the school grounds. "What do you like?"

"I like dogs, brownies, and books." Sanya answered, falling in step beside her.

"I love cats, chips, and watching TV," Tonya said. "Wait!"

Tonya's feet stopped. She looked disappointed, "These are complete opposites. We have nothing in common!"

Sanya thought about it, smiled, and said, "You could show me an episode of your favorite show, and I'll read you my favorite book. Deal?"

Tonya grinned and jutted out her hand. "Deal!" The girls shook hands.

When they got back inside, Sanya and Tonya were talking and laughing. "You sure became good friends!" Mrs. Violet observed. The girls nodded happily.

After school, Sanya asked Tonya, "Do you want to come to my house for a playdate sometime?" Tonya said, "I would love to!"

***

At home, Mom asked Sanya, "Did you have a good day today?"

Sanya raised her fists and said, "I had a hope-filled day. I cannot wait for tomorrow!"

5 COMMENTS…

A few weeks later, when Sanya was eating Banana chips after school, her mom brought in the mail. "I have good news for you."

Sanya clapped her hands, excited. "What is it?! Is it the Nintendo I have been asking for?"

"Try again."

"The puppy I wanted?" Sanya rubbed her hands.

"Hmm, let's just call this news," Mom said with a guilty chuckle. "Your glasses came in today." Mom said. The baby cooed loudly.

"You are right, Dev! It's just news. Not even okay news." Sanya made a face.

Sanya opened the box to find a pair of dark-colored glasses. It was a surprise when the eye doctor told them she was short-sighted and needed glasses. She had picked out those glasses after trying on so many. She was so excited when they had ordered them…but now that she had them in hand…

... What if kids at school made fun of her? Would she look too different now? Great! Another new thing to worry about.

Already, Phoenix annoyed Sanya every moment they crossed paths. Phoenix was this perfect girl, the school's star soccer player, and all the teachers loved her.

Except, she wasn't very nice when the adults weren't around. Sanya's mom had said it was sad that Phoenix felt the need to look down on others to feel better. It didn't help the situation...

One day on the bus, Phoenix asked, "Is your name Sonya, Saaneeeyaa, or maybe Saanjay? What does it even mean?"

Another day, at lunch, when she saw Sanya's lunchbox, it was, "Don't you only eat rotis all the time?"

Yet another day, while they were in line at the gym, Phoenix said, "Look how much taller I am than you!"

Today, she took the cake by simply not giving her the soccer ball during gym, saying, "Why don't you go play cricket? I hear that is big in India."

It wasn't just what she said, but the way she said it that made Sanya's ears burn and heart ache. Sanya bravely stood her ground each day, ignoring her, and often said, "Whatever, Phoenix!" Every day she wondered what she had ever done to Phoenix.

The only silver lining was that Phoenix seemed to know a lot about Indian culture. That was something to be happy about!

6 GLASSES…

"There go my dreams of becoming a pilot!"

"What do you mean?" Mom asked.

"Short-sighted people cannot see far, right?!" Sanya wailed.

Mom smiled and rubbed Sanya's back. "I don't think that's true, beta."

"Why do I need glasses at all? Why can't I have 20/20 vision like other kids?"

Mom sat down and pulled Sanya on her lap. She patted Sanya's hair, "It's like you said, darling. It's just luck. Sometimes, it's genes, and sometimes, it's our bodies. The good thing is that your glasses help you see the world as it is. Imagine those people who cannot be helped, even with devices or assistance."

Sanya nodded. "I guess."

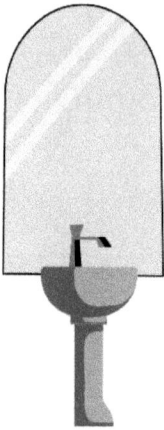

"Go put them on. See how they look."

Sanya went to the mirror in her bathroom and put on her glasses. She did like them! She walked out and looked around the living room and out the windows.

"Wow! Everything is so much clearer now, Mom! It used to be so fuzzy." Sanya looked around with amazement.

Mom smiled and said, "The glasses are part of you now." Sanya went back to the

26

restroom and smiled at herself in the mirror and nodded smartly. "Seeing clearly is certainly better than worrying about what others think."

Sanya came out and bent down to where Dev was playing with blocks on the floor. The baby stretched out to touch the glasses on Sanya's face. "Why thank you, Dev! These are new."

The baby giggled as his fingers spread over her face and glasses. "Eww! Dev!"

She took them off and cleaned them. "Smudges kind of beat the purpose of seeing clearly, lil bro."

7. SUPPORT...

The next day, at school, Phoenix didn't even wait for Sanya to enter the classroom.

"Short and four eyes, too!" Phoenix pointed at Sanya and snickered, standing in the corridor. Her friends around her giggled.

Sanya felt everyone staring. Her heart was beating so loud, she was scared everyone could hear it. She looked at Phoenix with defiance, "What great observation you have!"

Phoenix smirked, "Yes, hard to miss those extra eyes on your face, right?"

Before Sanya could say anything else, Tonya barged up to Phoenix and said. "I'm sorry, but I think you are confused, thinking that constantly commenting on people is a good joke! What do you gain from bullying people?"

Phoenix took a step back, "I'm not *bullying* anyone."

"No?"

"No!"

"Well, let me tell you. Constantly commenting on someone the way you do *is* a form of bullying. You can be suspended if we complain to the teacher or principal about it."

Phoenix looked around for support. When none came forward, she mumbled, "Jeez, someone is cranky today!" and walked away.

"Thanks Tonya. It was so brave of you to do that for me."

Tonya smiled sheepishly, "It wasn't easy, but she has been at this for days.

Someone else had to speak up for you. You standing up alone was not working!"

Sanya touched her glasses. "Do *you* think I look weird?"

"Are you kidding!? You look fabulous! So stately." Tonya said, observing Sanya's face closely with a hand on her hip.

Sanya giggled. "*Stately*! Where did you learn that word?"

Tonya thought about it, "Hmmm, I'm not sure. Maybe on one of the princess shows when I was a kid."

Sanya laughed out loud. "Are you a grandma *now*?"

Both girls started laughing and walked back into class.

After school, Tonya asked, "It's Friday! How about we go to the park today?"

8 PLAY…

The girls had just entered the park when Sanya groaned. Tonya looked at her, "What's wrong?"

"Phoenix is here," Sanya whined, stomping her foot. She rubbed her hands on her shorts.

"Why did the Math book not want to go to the playground?" Tonya asked.

Sanya looked at her blankly.

"It had too many problems with those already on it."

Sanya laughed despite herself and said, "It's okay. It's a big park, I guess. We can play in the sand pit on the opposite side."

"That's the spirit!" Tonya patted Sanya's back and they went off.

The girls were making holes in the sand in the volleyball court when they heard a loud "Woah!"

They turned toward the sound and saw Phoenix on the ground, face down. It looked like she had fallen chasing one of the boys she was playing with.

Her friends stood shocked. Suddenly, a couple started laughing. Phoenix was looking close to crying.

Sanya ran to her on instinct. "Are you hurt badly? Here." She gave Phoenix a hand to help her up.

"Huh?" Phoenix was so surprised she forgot her scraped knee and looked up at Sanya in wonder. She asked, "Why are you being so nice to me?"

"Because Kindness is not reserved only for nice people," Sanya said with a raised eyebrow.

Phoenix was speechless.

"Well, what do you know? You know how to be quiet too." Sanya teased. Phoenix smiled back, took Sanya's hand, and stood up.

Sanya continued. "It's easy to be kind! That boy is helping his grandmother walk, that girl is giving water to her pet, and Tonya is playing with that baby she has never met."

They looked on as Tonya played peek-a-boo with a cute little baby girl in stroller.

"Want to play with us?" Sanya asked Phoenix.

"Sure, let me go get my friends. Do you know how to play Kick the Can?"

When Sanya shook her head, Phoenix rubbed her hands and continued, "You are in for a treat." Tonya and Sanya made a lot of new friends that day.

9 SADNESS…

The clouds were dark and menacing. The air was getting chilly. The leaves were falling. Sanya had been missing her old neighborhood and friends. They used to have a huge block party for Halloween. It looked like the celebrations here would be just blah!

At school, things got worse when Sanya and Tonya got into a heated argument in Math class about a project they were working on to show the use of decimals.

It started with not agreeing on how to do the project to loud voices. Suddenly,

Sanya yelled, "You don't know what you are talking about. You don't even get good grades!"

@!#;

Tonya stood there with her mouth open. Mrs. Violet said quietly, "Sanya, that was uncalled for. You need to say sorry to Tonya."

Tears rose in Tonya's eyes, but Sanya wouldn't back down. She wasn't wrong. Tonya should have listened to her ideas. She sat down angrily, crossing her arms across her chest.

"Sanya, go to the principal's office," Mrs. Violet said.

The principal, Mrs. Brownle looked at Sanya from across her desk. She asked her questions about what happened and waited a few moments before talking, "Our words have power, Sanya."

"I know, Mrs. Brownle." Sanya said, sadly.

"Why, then, did you refuse to apologize?"

Sanya replied. "I *am* better at math than Tonya. She only gets Bs or Cs. What I said was not wrong."

Mrs. Brownle steepled her fingers together. "Just because a child is good at one thing doesn't mean they are bad at everything, correct?"

Sanya kept quiet, looking down.

"We work on projects together to use each other's strengths to bring out the best version of what we are working on."

Sanya kept looking down.

"I have noticed you and Tonya are friends. Can you tell me what is special about Tonya?"

Sanya immediately said, "Tonya makes the best brownies. She is also learning ballet and is very good at it."

"Dancing and baking both require subjects like math, physics, and thinking. Would you say that Tonya is not smart then?"

"No," Sanya said quickly.

"I think you already know what you need to do."

Sanya nodded and got up to leave.

"Also, something to think about, dear. Even if a weakness exists, pointing it out is often hurtful." Sanya paused at the door and thought back to Phoenix's comments.

10. EXAMPLE...

A week later, Dad was making Paneer Parathas for breakfast. He said, "I should have woken up early. I am running so late today."

The clouds outside were gray and Sanya's mood gloomy. Days had passed, and Sanya hadn't apologized to Tonya. They exchanged quick glances at lunch or recess but wouldn't speak to each other.

Sanya was having a paratha with curd when Mom walked in and asked Dad to hold the baby. Dad snapped, "Can't you see I am doing something?"

Mom pursed her lips and put the baby on the couch opposite the dining room. "Keep an eye on Dev, Sanya. I'll be back in a moment." Mom's voice was cold. She returned to the room with the baby's diaper and quietly started changing the baby Dev.

Dad closed the casserole with the parathas, wiped the counter, and approached Mom, hugging her from behind. "Here let me do it. I'm so sorry for what I said. The way I said it. Go eat. There's Chai too."

Mom turned, got up, and smiled. She touched his arm and said, "It's okay. Thank you for taking care of breakfast."

Saying sorry is as easy as saying thank you, Sanya thought.

That afternoon, Sanya walked up to Tonya at recess. "I'm sorry."

"For what?" Tonya asked, testily. It looked like she wanted to say more, but she paused. Instead, she said, "I can't believe you would say that to me."

44

Sanya didn't know what to say. This was more difficult than she thought.

"Whatever! I need some space anyway." Tonya said and walked away.

Sanya was taken aback. She didn't want more space. She just wanted the old Tonya back!

11. BEGINNING…

A couple of days later, Mom and Dad were packing parcels for customers. Sanya was reading on the sofa near them, while Dev played near her.

A little while later, she got restless and picked Dev onto her lap. The baby gurgled, stretching out his hands into Sanya's long hair. Sanya giggled.

"No, I don't need to cut my hair, silly! It's fine as it is. "

Suddenly, the baby bopped and toppled to the side. Sanya caught him in time, "Sorry, sorry."

The baby's wide eyes crinkled in the corners, and he smiled.

"Sigh! It's so easy with babies. Friends are so much harder, right!"

Dev smiled wider." You are right, Dev! It's harder, not impossible."

Sanya bounced Dev on her lap, but Dev reached for the pillow beside them and fell again. Sanya sighed, "But what do you know!" Sanya wondered if she should try again.

A few days later, Sanya had an idea. She caught Tonya while heading out to recess at the door. "Hey!"

"Hey."

"Look! I am sorry. It was not nice what I did. I did not mean what I said. I don't know. I thought about it. I guess when we aren't feeling good, we sometimes overreact and take it out on others and that is certainly not fair. Can you please forgive me?"

When Tonya kept looking away, Sanya continued. "If you forgive me, I promise not to boss you around on any future projects we do together."

"Seems impossible." Tonya shrugged and, a moment later, grinned.

Sanya crossed her heart. "I promise."

Tonya waved her hand. "It's okay."

"It's not okay, and I promise I will not do it again." Sanya held out a bracelet she had woven for Tonya. "Here, I made this for you."

Tonya took it: "Thank you. It's so pretty. Do you want to walk around the track?"

"Sure. I thought you would never talk to me again," Sanya said, kicking the dirt.

"I needed some time to miss you, I suppose." Tonya held out her hand. Sanya took it and shook it slowly and then hard. Tonya giggled, pushing Sanya, and yelled, "You are it!"

12. ADVENTURES…

Sanya and the family were playing a card game together in their PJs when Dad asked, "So, how's the new school and city working out for you, beta?"

Sanya put down a Reverse card, "There are good and bad days, but mostly good."

Mom asked, "Is that so?"

"Yes, sometimes one must go backwards or a little low to win like saying sorry to a friend or when I got that F in Science, I had to study again for the re-test, but it's all good as long as I stay positive about it."

Dad laughed, "There have been a lot of new beginnings this year, and you have been such a champ. We are so proud of you."

Sanya jumped onto her knees and said, "And guess what?!"

"What?" Mom asked.

"Tonya, Phoenix, and I will go trick-or-treating in *Phoenix's* neighborhood this year. We will plan our costumes next week."

Mom and Dad looked at each other and smiled.

"Here's to new starts - in life, friendships, school, and family too!" Sanya winked, grinning at Baby Dev before putting down a Draw +4 card.

Dad groaned dramatically. Mom snorted, and Sanya fell over laughing.

A few moments later, Sanya jumped up and yelled, "Look! Look!" Mom and Dad turned.

Baby Dev was walking, holding the coffee table.

Sanya held out her hands, and Baby Dev walked into them. "Baby Dev's first steps."

Sanya smiled, "You are right, Dev. You can come trick or treating with us this year too. New beginnings can mean new adventures."

"And a lot more babyproofing for us," Mom sighed happily, reaching for the camera.

"AND a lot more candy for me!!" Sanya grinned. When her parents looked surprised, she explained, "Baby Dev knows too much candy is not good for him. He says he will give half his candy to me."

Mom and Dad laughed. Sanya hugged her baby brother tightly.

THE END

GLOSSARY

dosa - A dosa is a thin, savory crepe in South Indian cuisine made from a fermented batter of ground white gram and rice. Dosas are served hot, often with chutney and a lentil curry called Sambhar

babbled - Talk fast and in a silly way, hard to understand

exaggerated – Expressing something in a larger, or worse than it really is

turmeric milk – Yellow turmeric mixed into (usually warm) white milk

chaos - A state of lot of mess

engulf - Surround or cover it completely

contradictory – Showing or saying that opposite things are true

wail – To express sorrow in a loud voice

cricket - Cricket is played with a bat and ball and involves two competing sides (teams) of 11 players

steepled – Make a pyramid like formation, like a steeple

GLOSSARY (contd.)

20/20 vision – A term used to express clear vision at a distance of 20 feet

defiance - A refusal to obey something or someone

stately – An old way of saying fancy or royal in some way

instinct – Your natural reaction to things

chai – The word chai means "tea" in Hindi. Made in many ways but often with ½ cup water, adding spices and tea leaves, boiling and then adding ½ milk till it almost boils over

paneer - Indian cheese that's made from souring with an acidic ingredient like lemon juice

parathas – A flat, thick piece of unleavened bread fried on a pan, usually stuffed with some other ingredients like spiced cottage cheese, potatoes, etc

testily – Angrily, or in an irritated way

rotis – Flat breads made with round pieces of whole wheat flour, cooked on a griddle

self-consciously – being nervous worrying about others opinion about you

Conversation Starters

1.Sanya pretends to know what her brother says in baby language. Have you ever enjoyed pretending?

2.Why do you think Sanya spoke to her teacher more "loudly and brightly "than she meant to?

3.What do you find *contradictory i*n your world today?

4.Sanya feels kids judging her clothes and choices. Do you think people around us judge us?

5.Sanya does a breathing exercise when she feels overwhelmed. What do you do?

6.Do you know the difference between short-sighted and long-sighted vision?

7.Phoenix asks Sanya her name's meaning. Do you know the meaning of your name?

8.Phoenix *seems* has a good knowledge of Indian culture. What stereotypes have you come across about cultures?

9.Sanya says something she later regrets. Have you ever said something you felt bad about later?

10.What do you think makes for a sincere way to tell someone you are sorry?

11.Sanya feels Home is where she has friends, and she is accepted as she is. What do you think home means?

ACVITIY TIME

In the book you see that saying things in anger or commenting on something else can be hurtful. What are some things that one can say to another to make them feel good about themselves?

Here are some more examples –

- "You're so good at sharing."
- "I admire how you never give up."
- "You're really good at [specific activity or skill]."

Now can you think about things you can say to yourself to make yourself feel better?

Can you think of reasons saying positive things is good for yourself and others?

KICK THE CAN RULES

It is a fun game where you and your friends try to avoid being caught by one person who is "it." Here's how it works:

- You need a can (or any other object that's easy to kick) and some friends to play with.
- One person is chosen to be "it," and they must close their eyes and count while the other players hide.
- While "it" is counting, everyone else hides. Once "it" finishes counting, they start searching for the other players.
- If "it" finds someone hiding, they shout out that person's name and the hiding spot. Then, both race back to the can.
- If the person hiding can kick the can before "it" does, everyone who's been caught gets to go free and hide again. But if "it" kicks the can first, the person found becomes "it" for the next round.

It's all about hiding, sneaking, and trying to outsmart the person who's "it"! Ready to play?

Would you like to know what happens next in Sanya's World? **Register to be an early reader** for a sneak peek at the next story at - **RaisingWorldChildren.com**

Thank you for leaving a kind review for this book on Amazon/GoodReads/your social media.
Feel free to tag - @raisingworldchildren

More books for finding belonging within -

PICTURE BOOKS

Ameya's Two Worlds
How Our Skin Sparkles
Sparkles of Joy
Small or Tall, We Sparkle After All
The Sparkles Within

ACTIVITY BOOK

Sparkles of Joy Activity Book

BILINGUAL BOOKS

Kya Kyaa Kare (What does K do?)
Muhaavare Aur Hum (Idioms and Us)
Humaare Tyohaar Series (Our Festivals)

BOOKS FOR ADULTS

Strong Roots Have No Fear
Raising the Global Mindset
Within

ABOUT THE AUTHORS

Aditi W. Singh is a multi-award-winning, bestselling author of twelve inclusive books rooted in modern values and Indian heritage. She founded **RaisingWorldChildren.com**, an in-print and online collaborative platform for diverse voices raising inclusive stories and sharing parenting tips. Raised in Kuwait, Aditi knows firsthand the need for stories that help prevent bullying and build self-confidence in third-culture kids. In addition to writing, she supports other authors by providing editing and coaching services to reach their publishing goals. She also has a love of teaching dance and creative writing.

Sharvi S. Singh, the inspiration and co-author of this book is first a budding fashionista and baking enthusiast. At just 10 years old, Sharvi's curious mind and kindness form the foundation of her mother's work. Her questions and insight often spark inspiration in her mother's writing, adding depth and authenticity to their lived stories. With her boundless energy and unwavering determination, Sharvi Singh is not just shaping the future but also leaving a colorful mark on the world.

www.ingramcontent.com/pod-product-compliance
Lightning Source LLC
Chambersburg PA
CBHW060710030426
42337CB00017B/2832